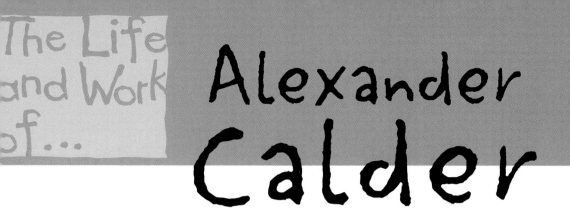

# The Life and Work of...

# Alexander Calder

Adam Schaefer

Heinemann Library
Chicago, Illinois

© 2003 Reed Educational & Professional Publishing
Published by Heinemann Library,
an imprint of Reed Educational & Professional Publishing,
Chicago, Illinois

Customer Service 1-888-454-2279

Visit our website at www.heinemannlibrary.com

Text designed by
Printed in

07 06 05 04 03
10 9 8 7 6 5 4 3 2 1

**Library of Congress Cataloging-in-Publication Data**
Schaefer, A. R. (Adam Richard), 1976-
     Alexander Calder / Adam Schaefer.
         p. cm. -- (The Life and work of--)
     Summary: Briefly examines the life and work of the twentieth-century American sculptor, describing and giving examples of his art.
     Includes bibliographical references and index.
     ISBN 1-40340-287-6 -- ISBN 1-40340-493-3 (pbk.)
     1. Calder, Alexander, 1898-1976--Juvenile literature. 2.
Sculptors--United States--Biography--Juvenile literature. [1. Calder, Alexander, 1898-1976. 2. Artists. 3. Art appreciation.] I. Title. II.Series.
NB237.C28 S33 2003
709'.2--dc21                                                    2002004012
     [B]                                                              CIP

**Acknowledgments**

Cover photograph: Art Resource

pp. 4, 22, 24, 25, 27, 28 Pedro E. Guerrero; p. 5 MoMA/Scala/Art Resource; pp. 6, 8, 16, 19, 20, 21 Art Resource; p. 7 Peter E. Juley & Son Collection/National Museum of American Art/Smithsonian Institution; p. 9 Courtesy Stevens Institute of Technology; p. 10 National Portrait Gallery/Smithsonian Institution/Art Resource; p. 11 General Research Division/New York Public Library/Astor, Tilden and Lenox  Foundations; p. 12 Hulton Archive/Getty Images; p. 13 Photo Alexander Kertesz/Ministere de la Culture—France; p. 14 Whitney Museum of American Art, New York; p. 15 LeeEwing/Archives of American Art/Smithsonian Institution; p. 17 Philadelphia Museum of Art; pp. 18, 26 Bettmann/Corbis;  p. 23 Jerry L. Thompson/Collection of Whitney Museum of American Art, New York; p. 29 Ezra Stoller/Esto Photographics, Inc.

All reproductions courtesy of the ©2002 Estate of Alexander Calder/Artists Rights Society (ARS), New York

Photo research by Alan Gottlieb

Some words in this book are in bold, **like this**. You can find out what they mean by looking in the Glossary.

# Contents

# Who Was Alexander Calder?

Alexander Calder was an American artist.
He made drawings, paintings, and **sculptures**.

*Lobster Trap and Fish Tail,* 1893

Calder is best known for his work as a **sculptor**. He made giant sculptures. He also invented **mobiles**. Mobiles are a kind of sculpture with moving parts.

# Early Years

Alexander Calder was born July 22, 1898, in Lawnton, Pennsylvania. His mother was a painter. His father and his grandfather were both **sculptors.** He had one sister.

*Laughing Boy,* 1910

Alexander was called "Sandy" by his friends and family. Sandy's father made this **sculpture** of Sandy when he was 12 years old. Sandy started to draw and make sculptures, too.

# Becoming an Engineer

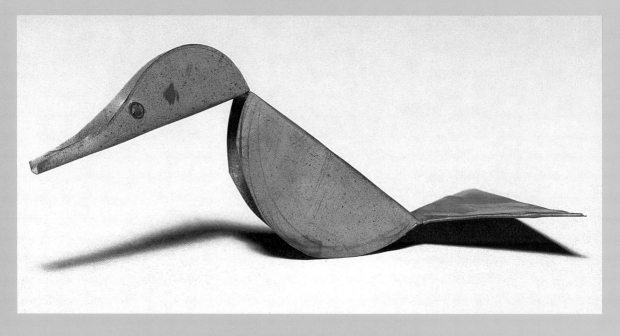

*Duck*, 1909

Sandy was always interested in building things. He was always taking things apart and using the pieces for different projects. He made this **sculpture** of a duck when he was 11 years old.

Sandy went to college at Stevens Institute of
Technology, in New Jersey. He learned how to
build things, and studied to be an **engineer.**
He left college, and worked as an engineer.
But he wanted to be an artist.

# Becoming an Artist

Sandy studied at the New York Art Students League for four years while he was working as an **engineer**. His work as an engineer would help him with his **sculptures** later in life.

*Self-Portrait,* 1925

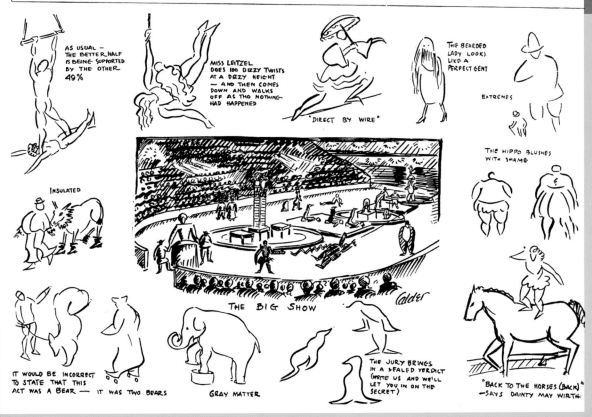

*Seeing the Circus with "Sandy" Calder*

While he studied at the Art Students League, Sandy worked as an **illustrator**. In 1925, he did some drawings of a circus for the *National Police Gazette*. Sandy enjoyed drawing the animals and the circus actors.

# Studying in Paris

In 1926, Sandy went to Paris, France. He worked with other artists, **sculptors,** and writers. He started working on a project.

Sandy made **sculptures** of circus animals and actors out of wire, wood, and cloth. He acted out circus scenes, and gave his figures voices. People all over Paris came to see his circus performances.

# Starting Sculpture

*Lion and Lion Tamer from Calder's Circus, 1926–1931*

The circus was **popular** in Paris. Sandy decided to go back to the United States to show his circus. People in the U.S. liked the circus too.

*Action Toys brochure*

Sandy wanted to make more **sculptures**.
Sandy needed to make money. He got a job
designing toys for a company in Wisconsin.
The toys were like his circus figures. He used
wire and wood to make animals that moved.

# Abstract Art

*Medusa*, 1930

Sandy's toys looked like real animals. He started to make wire **sculptures** that looked like real people. Art that looks like real things is called **representation**.

**16**

*Red Frame (Construction)*, 1932

Art that does not look like something real is called **abstract**. Sandy decided to make abstract sculptures. He cut wood and bent wire into strange shapes. This was a big change in Sandy's art.

# Paintings in Motion

Sandy liked his **abstract sculptures**. He also liked the way his circus figures and toys could move. He said that he wanted to put "paintings in **motion**." He attached an engine to this sculpture to make it move.

*Untitled,* 1942

Sandy wanted to find other ways to make sculptures move. He made sculptures to hang from the ceiling. The shapes in the sculptures moved and changed positions in the wind. These new sculptures were called **mobiles.**

**19**

# A New Sculpture

Sandy began spending time in both France and the United States. He had homes and art **studios** in both countries. This photograph shows Sandy in his studio in France.

*Five Swords,* 1976

Sandy was pleased with his **mobiles**. He started to make new sculptures called **stabiles**. Stabiles were big **sculptures**. They did not move. They looked different from different directions as people walked around them.

# New Combinations

In 1931, Sandy married Louisa James. Sandy and Louisa had two daughters named Mary and Sandra. Sandra grew up to be an artist like Sandy.

*Indian Feathers,* 1969

Sandy combined two of his art forms. He put
a **mobile** on top of a **stabile**. He called these
standing mobiles. Moving parts of a mobile
were attached to a base that did not move.

**23**

# A Happy Life

Sandy continued to work as he got older.
He still traveled back and forth between the
U.S. and France. His family would go with him.
In this picture, Sandy is working in his **studio**
in France.

**24**

Sandy did not make much money while he was alive, but he said he was always a happy person. He was happy making art. He was happy spending time with his wife, daughters, and grandchildren.

# Art Outside

*Flamingo,* 1974

As he got older, Sandy's work got bigger. He started making giant pieces of art for outside in city squares. Sandy would plan the **sculptures** in his **studio.** Then the sculpture would be put together outside. This sculpture is in Chicago, Illinois.

**26**

Sandy had to order materials from **factories** for his large sculptures. One of Sandy's sculptures in Italy is 60 feet tall. He had to visit an iron factory to get metal pieces big enough to make the sculpture.

# Last Exhibition

Alexander Calder died on November 11, 1976, at his daughter's home in New York City. He was still working very hard. He died at the same time as his work was shown in an **exhibition** in New York.

*Untitled,* 1976

One of the last **sculptures** he completed was
a giant **mobile** for the National Gallery, in
Washington, D.C. Sandy's sculptures are in
public places all over the world.

# Timeline

1898      Alexander Calder born, July 22

Spanish American War

1914–18 World War I

1915–19 Sandy studies at Stevens Institute of Technology in New Jersey.

1923      Sandy studies at the Art Students League in New York and does illustrations for the *National Police Gazette.*

1926      Sandy's first book, *Animal Sketching,* is published.

1930      Sandy performs his circus in Paris.

1931      Marries Louisa James

1932      Exhibits his **mobiles** for the first time

1938      Moves into large **studio** in Connecticut

1939–45 World War II

1958      Completes mobile *The Spiral* for the UNESCO building in Paris

1964      Major **exhibition** at Guggenheim Museum in New York

1976      Alexander Calder dies, November 11

# Glossary

**abstract**  art that does not look like something real

**engineer**  person who designs and makes things to do a certain job

**exhibition**  show of works of art in public

**factory**  place where things are made

**illustrator**  person who makes art to go with a story or poem

**mobile**  statue that is made of pieces that move

**motion**  changing position, moving

**popular**  liked by lots of people

**representation**  art that shows the way things look in real life

**sculptor**  person who makes sculptures or carvings

**sculpture**  statue or carving

**stabile**  statue that does not move but looks different from different directions

**studio**  place where an artist works

# Index

## More Books to Read

Lipman, Jean, and Margaret Aspinwall.
*Alexander Calder and his Magical Mobiles.* New York:
Hudson Hills Press, 1981.

Pekarik, Andrew. *Sculpture.* New York: Hyperion
Books for Children, 1992. An older reader can
help you with this book.

Venezia, Mike. *Alexander Calder.* Danbury, Conn.:
Children's Press, 1998. An older reader can help
you with this book.

## More Artwork to See

*Teodelapio.* 1962. Spoleto, Italy.

*Man.* 1967. Montreal, Canada.

*La Grande vitesse.* 1969. Vandenburg Center.
Grand Rapids, Michigan.

*Grand Crinkly.* 1971. Seoul, Korea.

*Four Arches.* 1975. Los Angeles, California.